Making Vision Stick

Also by Andy Stanley

MAKING
VISION STICK

ANDY
STANLEY

ZONDERVAN®

WILLOW
Willow Creek Resources

ZONDERVAN.com/
AUTHORTRACKER
follow your favorite authors

ZONDERVAN®

Making Vision Stick
Copyright © 2007 by Andy Stanley

Requests for information should be addressed to:
Zondervan, *Grand Rapids, Michigan 49530*

Library of Congress Cataloging-in-Publication Data

Stanley, Andy.
   Making vision stick / Andy Stanley.
     p. cm. — (Leadership library)
   ISBN-13: 978-0-310-28305-8
   ISBN-10: 0-310-28305-1
   1. Christian leadership. 2. Leadership—Religious aspects—Christianity. I. Title.
   BV652.1.S687 2007
   253—dc22   2007012719

This edition printed on acid-free paper.

Scripture quotations marked NIV are taken from the *Holy Bible, New International Version*®. NIV®. Copyright © 1973, 1978, 1984 by International Bible Society. Used by permission of Zondervan. All rights reserved.

Interior design by CHANGE Design Group

Printed in the United States of America

---

07 08 09 10 11 12 13 • 10 9 8 7 6 5 4 3 2 1

LEADERSHIP LIBRARY

The purpose of the Leadership Library is to provide leaders in all arenas—churches, businesses, schools, or nonprofits—with the cutting-edge thinking and the practical advice they need to take their leadership skills to the next level.

Books in the Leadership Library reflect the wisdom and experience of proven leaders who offer big insights in a pocket-size package. Whether you read these books on your own or with a group of colleagues, the Leadership Library presents critical insight into today's leadership challenges.

Making Vision Stick

I n February 2007, Starbucks Chairman Howard Schultz
sent a memo to his CEO, Jim Donald, that somehow
found its way onto the Internet and consequently onto
the computer screens of Starbucks fans everywhere. Three
people copied me on it in a single day.

In the memo, Schultz expresses concern that
his company has veered from its original charter. He
cites a series of internal decisions that eventually led to
a dilution of what customers had come to expect from a
visit to Starbucks. By unintentionally altering the Starbucks
experience, decision makers in the company had allowed
America's premier coffee-drinking environment to drift
from its mission. It was clear from the memo that this was

not simply a corporate concern. For Schultz it was personal. He urges his CEO to create a course that will lead Starbucks back to its original vision. This candid memo underscores the point of this little book and serves as a reminder that vision doesn't stick without constant care and attention.

One of the greatest challenges of leadership is making vision stick. Vision doesn't have much adhesive. Regardless of how clear I think I've made the vision and in spite of my commitment to repeat it often, someone will inevitably ask a question or offer a suggestion that makes me wonder, "Where have you been? Have you not been paying attention?"

When speaking to leaders on the subject of vision, I like to joke that the three primary obstacles to making vision stick are success, failure, and everything in between. There is no season in which a leader can push autopilot and expect the organization to remain vision-driven. It is possible for an organization to increase market share and profit margins while drifting from its original vision. I know from personal experience that it is possible for a church to grow numerically while drifting further and further away from the founding vision that energized the original team of leaders. The gravitational pull is always to the left or right of center. Success lures us into taking our hands off the wheel. Failure causes us to overcorrect. Both success *and* failure can lead to disaster.

The passage of time is hard on vision. Over time organizations become more complex. Complexity is distracting for leaders. Where there were once two balls to juggle, suddenly there are three, then four, and then forty. All of them are important. Where once there was one good opportunity to pursue, suddenly there are three. And each new opportunity leads to yet another and another. Complexity can kill the original vision.

General Motors is a good example. For over fifty years, GM dominated the American car industry with a market share that hovered at 50 percent. The architect of the vision that rejuvenated GM was Alfred Sloan. His idea back in 1924 was simple: Create five separate brands and price ranges for five distinct types of car buyers. Chevrolet was branded and priced for the first-time car buyer. Pontiac was branded and priced as an upgrade from a Chevrolet. From there a car buyer could upgrade to an Oldsmobile, then a Buick, and, finally, a Cadillac.

This approach took several years to catch on, but when it did, GM became king of the American car industry. Along with the growth of GM came unavoidable complexity. In the midst of the complexity, the simplicity and focus of the original vision were lost. The price points among brands

Vision is about what *could be* and *should be*, but life is about *right this minute*.

began to overlap. Before long, GM brands were competing with each other for the same customers. As brand clarity diminished, so did market share. Now a Chevrolet is anything from a $10,000 Aveo to a $60,000 Corvette. A Cadillac can be anything from a sports car to an SUV. As brand distinction diminished, so did market share. GM, the world's number one maker of cars and trucks, lost twenty points of U.S. market share in the last twenty-five years.

It's tough to make vision stick. Time has a way of eroding the adhesive. The forces that slowly eroded the adhesive of Alfred Sloan's vision for GM are working against you and your organization as well. Vision is about what *could be* and *should be*, but life is about *right this minute*. As important as we believe it is for people in our organizations to embrace our pictures of the future, their lives are consumed with the present. Life is about deadlines and decisions and problem solving, not to mention the kids and the house and the bills and the yard. To get people to sit still long enough to understand your vision is hard enough. But to get them to actually organize their lives around it is supremely difficult. The urgent and legitimate needs of today quickly erase our commitment to the *what could be* of tomorrow.

As the keeper of the vision, there's a lot working against you. Actually, it's worse than that. Just about everything is working against you. Success. Failure. Time. Life. But if, in spite of all that, there's something in you that refuses to give up and settle for the status quo, you may very well be the person God will use to bring about change. It's possible that God shares your anguish and your passion to make your vision stick.

In the following pages I'm going to download what I've learned over the last twenty years about making vision stick. This certainly isn't everything there is to know about this important subject. It's just all I know.

This is not a book about discovering or developing vision. My assumption is that you've done the difficult work of crafting a statement or paragraph that describes the preferred future for your organization. If not, you may want to dog-ear this page, gather your team, and spend the time necessary to develop a vision statement. If you've already done that, then let's figure out how to make your vision stick.

Taking Responsibility

When it comes to making your vision stick, here is the most important thing to remember: *You are responsible.* It is the leader's responsibility to ensure that people understand and embrace the vision of the organization. We are all tempted at times to blame the people around us for their inability to understand and act on the vision we have cast. But when a leader blames the follower for not following, the leader has ceased to lead. If the followers don't get it, we probably haven't delivered the vision in a way that makes it *get-able*. We are responsible for keeping the vision of our organization at the forefront. It is up to each one of us to make sure there is alignment between the activity and the vision of our enterprise.

While in graduate school, I had a professor who was fond of saying, "If the student hasn't learned, the teacher hasn't taught." The same could be said of leadership and casting vision. We are the keepers and purveyors of the vision. If the people around us don't know where we are going, it's because we haven't made it clear. Instead of casting stones, we need to look in the mirror and ask ourselves: How can I make the vision clearer? Simpler? More accessible? What can I do to make it stick? How do I drive this vision down into every level of the organization?

Once you have settled the issue of responsibility, here are five things you can do to significantly increase the adhesiveness of your vision.

1. State the vision simply.
2. Cast the vision convincingly.
3. Repeat the vision regularly.
4. Celebrate the vision systematically.
5. Embrace the vision personally.

State the Vision Simply

First, if your vision is going to stick in people's minds, it must be memorable.

I've talked to dozens of leaders who had an idea of what they wanted their organization to become, but it took them three paragraphs to explain it. They had a vision, but it wasn't one they could communicate effectively. People don't remember or embrace paragraphs. They remember and embrace sentences. As theologian Howard Hendricks said, "If it's a mist in the pulpit, it's a fog in the pew." If your vision is unclear to you, it will never be clear to the people in your organization. For your vision to stick, you may need to clarify or simplify it.

People don't remember or embrace paragraphs. They remember and embrace sentences. As theologian Howard Hendricks said, "If it's a mist in the pulpit, it's a fog in the pew."

It is better to
have a vision statement
that is incomplete and
memorable than to have
one that is complete
and forgettable.

When we launched North Point Community
Church, our vision was "to create a church that unchurched
people would love to attend." For the theologically astute,
a statement like that raises lots of questions. Admittedly, it
is void of theological content. There's nothing there about
life change or salvation. The statement is incomplete. But if
you wanted to know what we were about, that was it. We
were committed to creating a church for the unchurched
or, to use a phrase Bill Hybels coined, "irreligious people."
We were clear from the beginning that we were going after
a different market than the average church. When people

complained about what we did and didn't do compared to the other churches they had attended, we simply shared our vision. That answered most of the questions. And our vision statement galvanized our leadership around what was distinctive about our organization.

As you evaluate your vision statement, remember this: *It is better to have a vision statement that is incomplete and memorable than to have one that is complete and forgettable.* As a leader, you have endless opportunities to define terms and expand on concepts for the people who are intrigued enough to ask questions and gather more information. But you have limited opportunities to cast your vision to the drive-by audience, the people who may never give you their undivided attention, much less a second chance. For that group you need a statement that will stick.

Another example of a memorable vision statement is this one from Internet giant eBay: "to provide a global trading platform where practically anyone can trade practically anything." Note that the eBay vision statement doesn't even mention the Internet. And there's nothing in there about bidding on items. I don't know anyone who has ever *traded* anything on eBay. They usually *buy* things. This statement doesn't give you the full scope of what eBay is about. But it is intriguing and memorable. And for company insiders, the ones who are privy to the entire strategy, this simple statement is enough. It encapsulates pages of information and marketing strategies. More importantly, it summarizes the preferred future of the company.

Several years ago it occurred to the leadership team at North Point that we had accomplished what we had set out to do. We had successfully created a church that unchurched people loved to attend. By that time we had created a second and then a third campus modeled after the original church. All three have been successful at capturing the imaginations of unchurched people in their respective communities. Vision accomplished.

Our new vision revolves around connecting people into small groups. Our first vision statement said, "We envision fifty thousand people participating in weekly small groups that are committed to multiplying." Even though we had reduced our vision to a sentence, it was not catchy or memorable. So our groups director, Bill Willits, went back to his team and brainstormed how to make the vision easier to communicate. They came back with this: 5/50/10. Our vision is five thousand groups with fifty thousand people by 2010. 5/50/10.

It's been exciting to watch our various departments begin to reorganize around this new vision. One of the powerful things about a clearly articulated vision is that it has a way of redirecting the focus and resources within an organization. If the vision is too complicated for people to embrace, nothing changes. People tend to keep doing what they've always done the way they've always done it. Bottom line: to make vision stick, it needs to be easy to communicate.

Cast the Vision Convincingly

The second imperative to making vision stick is to cast it convincingly. Once you have your vision in a form that makes it easy to communicate, you must communicate it in a way that moves people to action. In this section I'm going to give you a simple formula that will help you communicate your vision convincingly. This is not original with me. I pulled it right out of the Old Testament from the book of Nehemiah.

Around 444 BC, a Jewish man named Nehemiah was charged with the task of rebuilding the wall around the city of Jerusalem after it had lain in ruins for over a hundred years. The Jews living in Jerusalem at the time were content to live with the broken-down wall. Nehemiah's compelling vision for their future changed their attitude. In this short but highly effective speech to the Jews still living in Jerusalem, we find a brilliant model for casting a compelling vision. As you read, look for three things: He defined the problem that his vision addressed.

He offered a solution. Then he followed with the reason why something had to be done and why it had to be done immediately.

> Then I said to them, "You see the trouble we are in: Jerusalem lies in ruins, and its gates have been burned with fire. Come, let us rebuild the wall of Jerusalem, and we will no longer be in disgrace." I also told them about the gracious hand of my God upon me and what the king had said to me.
>
> They replied, "Let us start rebuilding." So they began this good work. (Nehemiah 2:17–18 NIV)

1. Define the problem

To cast a convincing vision, you have to define the problem that your vision addresses. For Nehemiah the problem was obvious. Jerusalem was in ruins! That was a problem for the Jewish people. But it wasn't until he drew their attention to it and put forth a plan of action that they felt compelled to do something about it.

Every vision is a solution to a problem. If your vision doesn't get traction, something that needs to happen won't happen. A problem will continue to go unaddressed. To make your vision stick, your audience needs to understand what's at stake. It's the *what's at stake* issue that grabs people's hearts. Only a clear explanation of the problem will cause people to sit up and say, "Something must be done!" If your target audience doesn't know what's at stake, the vision will never stick.

So what problem does your vision propose to solve? Every successful organization—for profit or nonprofit—is viewed by its customers or clients as a solution to a problem. If you don't believe me, Google "business solutions." You'll get more than 440,000 results. Why? Because a business knows its future hinges on the perception that its product is a solution to someone's problem. The same is true of your vision. Buy-in by others hinges on your ability to convince them that you are offering a solution to a problem they are convinced needs to be solved.

To cast your vision in a convincing manner, you need to be able to answer these two questions: What is the need or problem my vision addresses? and What will happen if those needs or problems continue to go unaddressed?

2. Offer a solution

Your vision is a solution to a problem. When you link a problem that people are convinced needs to be solved with a clear and compelling solution, you have the potential to capture their hearts. Nehemiah's solution was pretty straightforward: "Come, let us rebuild the wall of Jerusalem." Reconstructing the wall was the solution to a problem.

Perhaps you are familiar with the ONE campaign. ONE is an effort to rally Americans in the fight against global AIDS and extreme poverty. Its vision statement is as follows: "ONE: The Campaign to Make Poverty History." This is an example of rolling both the problem and the solution into the vision statement. The problems are AIDS and extreme poverty. The solution, or vision, is to eliminate both.

Perhaps you read that and wonder, "But how? Who? Where? What's the plan?" Convincing vision statements never answer all those questions. That's what websites, newsletters, and speeches are for. The vision statement simply states the solution to a problem. The ONE campaign aims to end AIDS and extreme poverty. To make your vision casting convincing, you have to present your vision as the solution to a problem. What solution are you proposing? How is your organization positioned as a solution to a problem?

3. Present a reason

The third component to a convincing vision is the *reason* something must be done *now*. You have to present people with a reason for your vision. You have to answer the questions: *Why must we do this? Why must we do this now?*

Nehemiah's reason was wrapped up in this theologically pregnant phrase, "and we will no longer be in disgrace." Space does not allow me to fully explain the significance of those eight words. The bottom line: the Jews knew that the city of Jerusalem was meant to reflect the greatness of their God. As long as the city was in disarray, it reflected poorly on God. Something had to be done.

One problem we all wrestle with is that our visions are rarely new or unique. Like Nehemiah, we look at the things around us that need to change and we wonder, "Why hasn't somebody already done something about this?" We aren't the first to see that something needs to be done. But what others have seen and been content

You have to present people with a reason for your vision. You have to answer the questions: *Why must we do this? Why must we do this now?*

to ignore, a leader sees and takes action. A leader points the way to a solution and gives a compelling reason why something must be done now. In Nehemiah's case, the wall had been that way for over a hundred years. Why rebuild now? What had suddenly changed? Only one thing: a leader came along who saw and stated the problem of sticking with the status quo.

Consider the ONE Campaign. AIDS and extreme poverty aren't new. But as a result of the ONE Campaign, there are thousands of Americans doing something now who weren't doing something before, even though they were aware that something should be done. The ONE Campaign is providing thousands of Americans with a reason to act.

The original vision for the Willow Creek Association is another great example. Bill Hybels wasn't the first person to recognize that local churches were in trouble. That was old news. Bill was the leader who finally said, "Enough is enough, something must be done. And something must be done now!" It was his burden for the next generation of church leaders—guys like me—that compelled him to launch the Willow Creek Association. Its purpose: to provide local church leaders with strategic vision, training, and resources to build biblically functioning churches. In 1992, the Willow Creek Association was launched with a few Midwest churches. Today it includes a global membership of more than 12,000 churches. The WCA is a solution to a problem. The problem existed long before the WCA was formed. But the solution would have never gotten off the ground if Bill and his team had not cast a vision that included a reason why the problem could not be ignored for another generation.

Every organization—business, nonprofit, or church—was launched because somebody stumbled upon a reason why it was time to act. You weren't the first to recognize the problem. What makes you different is that you have decided to do something about the problem now.

As you think about your organization's vision, ask why act now? What's at stake now? Why not allow another year or two or ten to go by? What makes this season unique for you and your team? When you can answer these questions, you have created a context for the passion you will need to move people forward. They already know there's a problem. They probably have a hunch about the solution. What they need is someone to give them a reason to rise up and do something about it. That is the role of a leader. To cast your vision convincingly, you need a reason for why *now* is the time. If you haven't

They already know there's a problem. They probably have a hunch about the solution. What they need is someone to give them a reason to rise up and do something about it. That is the role of a leader.

defined the problem, determined a solution, and discovered a compelling reason why now is the time to act, you aren't ready to go public with your vision. It won't stick.

I'll make a prediction. If you and your team will set aside time to define the problem, state your vision as a solution, and discover a compelling reason why now is the time to act, you will walk away from that meeting, or series of meetings, with more passion for what you are about than you thought possible. Something will come alive in you. And when you talk about your vision, you will be more convincing than you've ever been before. Note too that when your team talks about the future, they will use similar terminology. You may even create a new vocabulary for your organization.

Repeat the Vision Regularly

Casting a convincing vision once is not enough to make it stick. Twice isn't enough either. Vision needs to be repeated regularly. To make it stick, you need to find ways to build vision casting into the rhythm of your organization. This is not difficult to do. But it is one of those things that won't happen without a leader intentionally taking action.

There are two strategic times when I regularly repeat the vision for all three of our campuses: January and May. Every January I preach a two- or three-part vision-casting series. I chose January because it is the month when everybody goes to church, regardless of what the topic is. Churches and health clubs do well in January. January is a strategic time for us because the draw is not the topic; the draw is the rhythm of life. People want to start the year off right, so in our part of the country, they go to church.

After the January series I often hear the comment, "That message sounded a lot like last year's January series." That observation is correct. Vision is a constant. Our vision has remained the same for ten years. For ten Januarys in a row, our people were presented with the same vision.

As committed as I am to the idea of casting vision on a regular basis, at times I feel a bit guilty. I feel like I'm repeating myself. "Surely they know all of this by now," I reason. But I go right ahead and do it anyway. Why? Because vision doesn't stick. Casting vision in January doesn't guarantee anything about our congregation's commitment to our vision the following January. And so I repeat it over and over.

The other strategic time for us is May because that is the month we enlist volunteers for the coming fall. Every May we build a weekend service around the value of volunteerism. It is a natural time to cast vision for what we are doing and why we need everyone to be involved. Vision casting in January and May is built into the rhythm of our organization. I don't have to remember to do it. The calendar dictates it.

Public presentations are just one way to communicate vision. By themselves, they are not adequate. I'm constantly looking for ways to reinforce where we are headed and how we plan to get there. In the past I've sent letters and e-mails to our congregation. But I've doubted the effectiveness of that form of communication, especially for something as important as vision. Vision should evoke emotion. And it's difficult to evoke emotion with an e-mail or a letter.

The other problem with a traditional letter, or even an e-mail, is that it may or may not be read. At best only one person in a household will read it. So recently I tried something new. I created an audio letter. Here's how it worked. I wrote out what I wanted to say and then recorded it. The recording was about twelve minutes long and included a soon-to-be-released worship song by one of our musicians. We made several thousand copies of the CD and gave one to every family on their way out of a weekend service. I asked them to listen to it in their cars on the way home with their families. We handed out the CDs for three weeks so that everybody had an opportunity to pick one up. The response was incredible. Not only did they receive the information, they *heard* the information. I was able to layer the content with emotion. Plus, the entire family could experience the content together, thus creating an opportunity for discussion. Discussion reinforces information. Early on I was concerned about the cost of creating that many CDs. I was relieved to discover that CD reproduction is so cheap that the cost of the entire project was almost the same as if I had mailed everyone a letter.

At some point you will need to determine the optimal times and contexts for vision casting in your organization. Look for ways to build it into your natural business or ministry cycle, into the rhythm of your organization. When are people most attentive? When is everybody there? When in the rhythm of organizational life do people need a reminder? Along with the timing issue, think through your available channels of communication. What opportunities exist that would allow you to push the vision further down into the organization? Are you making good use of company newsletters, websites, and intranet capabilities? Would an audio letter work in your context?

We all need to be reminded why we are doing what we are doing. We need to be reminded what's at stake. We need to be reminded of the vision.

Every organization is different, even though the people in every organization are pretty much the same. We all need to be reminded why we are doing what we are doing. We need to be reminded what's at stake. We need to be reminded of the vision. And we need it more often than most leaders realize.

Okay, let's review. To make vision stick, you need to *state it simply, cast it convincingly,* and *repeat it regularly.* The fourth imperative is that you must *celebrate it systematically.*

Celebrate the Vision Systematically

To make vision stick, a leader needs to pause long enough to celebrate the wins along the way. Celebrating the wins does more to clarify the vision than anything else. The tricky thing about vision is that it is made up of words and word pictures. There aren't any photographs. After all, vision is about the future. This makes it difficult for leaders to get everyone on the same page. When I talked about a church that unchurched people would love to attend, that conjured up all kinds of different images. How do I make sure that what I'm envisioning is the same thing the people around me are envisioning?

One way is to celebrate real-world events that illustrate what you envision. Build these events into the rhythm of your organization. I know from countless conversations that some leaders consider celebrations a complete waste of time. But when you celebrate the right things, you are using the most effective form of vision casting. Celebrations create the opportunity for an "a-ha" moment. "Oh, so that's what you're talking about." Celebrating a win incarnates the vision, bringing clarity in a way that words alone cannot.

Every organization celebrates something. But if your vision doesn't align with your celebrations, I assure you that what's celebrated will overpower the vision and determine the course of your organization. Here's an organizational principle you don't want to lose sight of: *What's celebrated is repeated.* The behaviors that are celebrated are repeated. The decisions that are celebrated

Here's an organizational principle you don't want to lose sight of: *What's celebrated is repeated.*

are repeated. The values that are celebrated are repeated. If you intentionally or unintentionally celebrate something that is in conflict with your vision, the vision won't stick. Celebrations trump motivational speeches every time.

Using Notes, Letters, and E-mails

In my world, I'm often made aware of our wins through letters and e-mails that come my way. A few years back, I received this e-mail from a woman in our church.

Dear Andy,

In your talk last Sunday, you spoke about the impact that small group leaders have on the children in their groups. I wanted to let you know about my son's small group leader who goes above and beyond normal expectations. My son Graham is in the fifth grade and his small group meets at the 8:30 hour. His small group leader is Greg Stubbs. As you know, Greg was called into active service as a part of the Iraqi Freedom mission. Greg was sent to Italy and then to Turkey and then to an aircraft carrier. But did that stop him from being concerned about the members of his small group? No. Greg sent e-mails

*from Turkey telling of the work he is doing and
asking about what the kids are doing. He even
went so far as to call Graham from Turkey.*

*When you think about all the things that were on
Greg's mind and then realize that he cares enough
about his small group members to keep in contact
with them from a war zone, it makes you stop and
think about the reasons we create not to keep
in touch with our own small group leaders and
members. We understand that Greg may be coming
home in the next couple of months and we will
certainly be ready to thank him for his service.*

For me, for our organization, that was a huge win.
We are constantly casting vision to our small group leaders
about how important it is to maintain a relationship with
their kids outside of Sunday morning. Here's a guy who
was so committed to his boys that he continued to stay in
touch from overseas while serving his country. That was
amazing. I knew this was a win we needed to celebrate.

When Greg returned from his tour of duty, I called
him and told him about the e-mail. Then I asked if I could

read it on the Sunday in May when I cast vision and recruit volunteers for the following ministry season. Greg agreed.

That morning I got up and talked about serving in the local church . . . like I've done for ten years. I reminded our congregation that our vision was to create irresistible environments for unchurched adults and their families. Toward the end I read the e-mail about the boy in Greg's small group. As you can imagine, everyone was moved.

What they didn't realize, however, was that Greg, in uniform, was sitting in the front row. At the end of the letter, I turned to him and said, "Greg, would you stand." People went crazy. Then I said, "For those of you who are too busy to serve because you have so many pressing things in your life, after the service I invite you to come and share your excuses with Greg." That year we needed at least 1,300 volunteers. Because of Greg's example, over 1,700 people volunteered to serve.

Greg was a living, breathing example of our vision for our children's small groups. Celebrating his commitment clarified for everyone exactly what we mean when we talk about laying a foundation for the next generation of kids. An e-mail like that doesn't come along every day. But when I get one, I look for ways to leverage it.

Reading an e-mail in church is a spontaneous way of celebrating vision. Effective, to be sure, but spontaneous. I imagine in your organization spontaneous things surface that serve as points of celebration. But for vision to stick, you need to develop systematic ways to celebrate your wins.

Our two primary contexts for celebrating our vision are our Monday morning all-staff meetings and our Sunday morning baptisms. At our all-staff meeting, I open with this question: "What happened last week that made you feel like you've made progress in your mission to lead people into a growing relationship with Christ?" Then I shut up and listen. For twenty or thirty minutes I let the staff tell stories. I use those stories as a time to reiterate: "That's our vision. That's why we do what we do. That's the bull's-eye on target. That's the win." Nothing gives definition to vision like pausing to celebrate a win.

The other built-in time to celebrate a win in our organization is during baptisms on Sunday mornings. We require everyone who wants to be baptized to come in a couple of weeks before and record a two- to four-minute video where they describe their faith journey. We play these videos in the service just before they are baptized. If you won't do the video, we won't baptize you. As you might imagine, we get some resistance. Most people don't relish the idea of having their faces plastered all over a giant screen. And speaking into a video camera is not the most comfortable thing to do either. To those who resist we explain, "This video is an opportunity for you to share your story with more people in one day than you will for the rest of your life."

I'm convinced that our baptisms do more to drive home our vision than anything else we do. It is one thing for me to say, "Our desire is to create environments where life change happens." It is quite another thing to hear someone's story of life change that started in one of our environments.

When I refer to this as a celebration, I mean that quite literally. People cheer, whistle, applaud, and at times come to their feet in response to what they see and hear. On one level they are celebrating the transformational power of God. At another level they are celebrating the success of what we have come together to do as a church. There are Sunday mornings when the video testimonies are so moving, I'm tempted to pray and dismiss.

Figure out how to build celebration into the rhythm of your organization. For your vision to stick, it must be celebrated. The people in your organization are already celebrating something. But if there is a disconnect between your vision and what's being celebrated, that's a dynamic that needs immediate attention.

To make vision stick, state it simply, cast it convincingly, repeat it regularly, and celebrate it systematically. The last imperative is *embrace it personally.*

Embrace the Vision Personally

Your willingness to embody the vision of your
organization will have a direct impact on your credibility
as a leader. Living out the vision establishes credibility
and makes you a leader worth following. When people are
convinced that the vision has stuck with you, it is easier
for them to make the effort to stick with the vision. Your
giftedness may enable you to gather a following. But it will
take more than talent to make your vision stick.

When you embody the vision of your organization,
people come to believe that your job is more than just a job
for you. Over time it occurs to insiders that you would be
doing the same thing even if there weren't an organization

> Living out the vision
> establishes credibility and
> makes you a leader worth following.
> When people are convinced that the
> vision has stuck with you, it is easier
> for them to make the effort to
> stick with the vision.

to support you. When it is evident to those closest to you that you have personally embraced the vision, you give them permission to do the same. At that point you're not leading from position—you're leading from influence.

When my wife, Sandra, and I bring an unchurched friend or family to a weekend service, I tell the staff about it on Monday morning. I thank them for partnering with my family to reach our community. I talk about our small group. I look for opportunities to talk about the difference our children's small groups are making on our kids. I want

> If you say you believe in something, live it out. And live it in a way that the people around you can see it. That's not arrogant. That's liberating.

them to know that this is personal for me. I believe. I'm in. This isn't just a job. It's a calling.

Embracing the vision personally isn't just a "ministry" value. Like you, I have friends who are fanatics about the products they sell or the companies they work for. My friends who work for Chick-fil-A insist on wearing company ties everywhere they go. My friends who work for Coke will have nothing to do with Pepsi products. My friend Al, who works for GM, is constantly asking me when I'm going to trade in my Toyota SUV for a Tahoe. When he heard that I couldn't get my vehicle started one morning, he was all over that. I won't even start on my PC friends who think my Mac is a toy. And that's how it should be. If you say you believe in something, live it out. And live it in a way that the people around you can see it. That's not arrogant. That's liberating. It frees others to join without reservation and without suspicion.

Let's face it. You can sniff out a phony a mile away. The people closest to you can as well. They will know if you are trying to leverage a vision just to get them to work harder, to grow for growth's sake, or simply to expand your personal fortune. Sharp people will not embrace a vision that is merely a marketing scheme for someone's personal agenda. I'm tempted to say that "no one" will follow a leader who doesn't live his or her vision. But the truth is, people do it all the time. Eventually they wake up to discover they've been used and deceived.

Certainly there are leaders who set out from the beginning to dupe people into following and believing a fabricated vision. But I'm convinced that most leaders are sincere in the beginning. They cast visions early on that they really do embrace. But over time they lose sight of the goal. They get distracted or bored. They continue to talk the talk publicly, but privately they are operating from an entirely different set of values. You don't want to end up there. You want the people who choose to follow you to

> You want the people
> who choose to follow you to
> end their journeys with more
> respect for you than when they
> began. For that to happen,
> you have to embrace and
> live out the vision.

end their journeys with more respect for you than when they began. For that to happen, you have to embrace and live out the vision.

Let's be honest. There are days, maybe even seasons, when you are not going to *feel* as passionate about your vision as you did in the early days. Success and failure, time and life are not only tough on vision, they are tough on leaders. As committed as I am to creating churches that unchurched people love to attend, there are times when I don't have any close friends who are unchurched. Don't tell my staff this, but there are times when I don't even *want* any friends who are unchurched. I have enough friends. I don't do a good job keeping up with the friends I have. Why would I want to add anyone else to the list?

Your context may be different than mine, but I'm sure there are times when you just don't *feel it* the way you once felt it. You are just as committed in your mind and heart as you've ever been. But you lack passion and you may find yourself losing interest.

Here's my advice for the leaders who've lost, or sense they are losing, their passion to live out their visions. Don't try to manufacture energy around something you

Everybody gets tired and distracted at times. Admitting it is healthy and will give your inner circle permission to admit it to you as well.

don't have energy for. The people closest to you will sense that in a heartbeat. They may not know exactly what's wrong. But they will know *something* isn't right.

Don't fake it. Admit it. If possible, admit it to some safe people within your organization. Tell them you have not abandoned the vision; you are just a bit vision weary. If they are honest, they will tell you they have felt . . . or are feeling . . . the same way. Everybody gets tired and distracted at times. Admitting it is healthy and will give your inner circle permission to admit it to you as well. When I feel like I'm losing my passion for what I believe God has called our church to do, I tell people and ask them to pray for me. When there are no unchurched people in my life, I tell my staff and ask them to pray. I think it is important for them to know that my passion comes and goes, but my commitment to what we are doing never wanes.

To make vision stick, we not only need to embrace it personally, we need to communicate it honestly. Let your staff know about your vision successes and your vision failures. Let them see your passion when it is hot. And even when you're running on fumes, let them know you are still committed. That kind of transparency builds trust. It will help ensure that your vision sticks!

Vision Slippage Indicators

If you state your vision simply, cast it convincingly, repeat it regularly, celebrate it systematically, and embrace it personally, you are well on your way to making your vision stick. However, it's always wise to be alert to signs that your vision has lost its adhesive. In this section I'm going to briefly discuss the six organizational warning gauges I keep my eye on. They are: new projects, new programs, new products, requests, stories, and complaints. Instead of addressing each of these individually, I've divided them into two groups of three each.

Projects, Products, and Programs

We've all heard and read stories about businesses that lost their focus, drifted away from their core competencies, and wound up in trouble. The same thing happens with churches and parachurch organizations. Vision drift is slow. In many cases, it begins with the introduction of something new to the organization: a new product, the acquisition of a new company, or the launch of a new initiative. In my world, it's usually the introduction of a new program.

Leaders must keep their antennae up for *new* things that have the potential to distract from the *main* thing. New projects, programs, or even products must

> Leaders must keep their antennae up for *new* things that have the potential to distract from the *main* thing. New projects, programs, or even products must be vision-centric.

be vision-centric. A good wordsmith or someone with a persuasive personality can make any project or program sound like it is within the scope of the vision, and that can be a problem. As a leader, you need to do the due diligence necessary to keep distracting elements out of the organization.

At North Point, there are a lot of things we don't do on purpose—not because they wouldn't be successful, but simply because they don't pass the vision test. Every year or so, someone will approach me with the idea of starting a Christian school. I'm all for Christian education. But I'm not for churches starting schools. The mission and vision of a school is different than that of a local church. At least I believe it is. To leverage the resources of a church to begin a school always interferes with the effectiveness of the church. My standard line is this: Schools are smarter than churches. You never hear about a school starting a church. People who start schools know there is a fundamental difference in focus and vision.

We've avoided launching a "sports ministry" as well. On several occasions, people have approached us who are ready to put up the money to help us build ball fields and gymnasiums. We have turned them down because a sports program is actually *counter* to our vision. One of the best ways for believers in our community to connect with unchurched people is through their children's recreational activities. Why would we bring all of that in-house and pull our folks out of the recreational parks and gyms in our community?

We have a phrase that reminds us to look at new ideas through the vision lens: "Think steps, not programs." Our vision is not a smorgasbord of programs. We want to help people take steps in their spiritual journeys. If a new idea provides a step in a specific direction, we will consider it. If not, we won't.

Our approach stands in stark contrast to a practice that many church leaders have adopted. I've actually heard this taught as a good approach to pastoral leadership. It goes something like this: "When somebody comes to you with a ministry idea, tell 'em, 'That's a great idea! Why don't you lead it?'" This is heralded as an effective way to involve people in ministry. I think it's a great way for a church to lose focus. Vision, not people's random ideas, should determine programming. Vision, not a cool PowerPoint presentation, should determine which new initiatives are funded by your organization. Vision, not the promise of great returns, should determine which products are launched.

To make sure your vision is not losing its adhesive, be on the lookout for new projects, programs, and products. Keep your eye on the new things that are trickling in. And while you're on the lookout for new things, there are three things you need to be listening to as well.

Requests, Stories, and Complaints

The questions people ask, the stories they tell or don't tell, and the things they complain about communicate a great deal about the stickiness of your vision. *Questions* communicate values. The questions you ask communicate what's most important to you. That's true of everybody. *Complaints* are like questions. They communicate what a person values. *Stories* are moments of spontaneous celebration. Requests, complaints, and stories reveal a great deal about what's on the minds and hearts of the people in an organization.

Consider this: If there was 100 percent buy-in to your vision by the people you work with, what questions would they ask? What kinds of stories would they feel compelled to tell? What would get on their nerves? Begin to listen. Really listen. If the people around you aren't asking the right questions, telling the right stories, or complaining about the right things, your vision may be slipping. Questions, stories, and complaints are context specific. The questions you are listening for will be different from the ones on my radar screen. The same is true of stories and complaints. These three expressions are important indicators in every environment.

I recently received a letter from a couple that has attended North Point for ten years. They wrote to express concern about our music. "We feel like the style and feel of the music has changed over the past several years," they said. They were exactly right. It has. What concerned me was that they didn't understand why. The vision had slipped. By their own admission, they started attending when they were single. Now they are married with kids. They are two stages of life away from when they first joined us. Our music is exactly where it was ten years ago in relation to culture, which is our goal. But they aren't where they were ten years ago. They were complaining about the wrong thing.

The week before that I received an e-mail asking why we didn't use more hip-hop. That was a good complaint. As music culture continues to move in that direction, we should too. The young woman who sent that e-mail understood our vision. What people complain about communicates their understanding of the vision.

> What people complain
> about communicates
> their understanding
> of the vision.

As I mentioned earlier, in our weekly staff meetings we give people opportunities to tell stories from the previous week. Those mini-celebrations tell me a great deal about what our staff sees as important. If they are willing to share stories in front of the entire group, they must believe their stories are relevant to our vision and mission. When there are no stories to tell, something's wrong. I also get concerned when the stories people tell are a celebration of something other than what we are about.

If you are in ministry, listen closely to the *questions people ask.* Listen closely to prayer requests.

If your ministry vision centers on engaging unbelieving people with the message of Christ, but 90 percent of the prayer requests from your leadership and staff are about sick people, your vision is slipping. We pray for what we are most burdened for. If nobody in my leadership circle requests prayer for someone who is far from God, that's a big red flag for me. That's a definite vision-slippage indicator. On more than one occasion, I've called a time-out to remind our leadership that we are not a hospital. I'm all for praying for the sick. But if that's the only group we are burdened to pray for, then perhaps we are the ones who need prayer! Perhaps the vision has slipped.

Every leader should identify gauges that measure the alignment between the organization's activity and its vision. Slippage is going to occur. There is no way to avoid it. Course corrections are a part of organizational life. The sooner you recognize the slippage, the sooner you can do something about it. Keep an eye on new projects, programs, and products. Keep your ears open to questions, complaints, and stories. These are dashboard warning indicators you cannot afford to ignore.

Living the Vision: A Personal Story

Maintaining vision is difficult, both organizationally and personally. As committed as I say I am to leading people into a growing relationship with Jesus Christ, it is easy for me to schedule that right out of my life. After all, like you, I'm busy. I'm real busy. If I'm not careful, all my time will be consumed with church and family. And while that may appear noble to some, it is not enough.

My wife, Sandra, and I are committed to developing relationships with unchurched people in our community. Our kids hear us pray at night for friends who are far from God. But there is a difference between being committed to something in your heart and being committed to it when the alarm clock rings on Monday morning. The day-to-day grind makes it hard to stay focused on the vision. This became all too apparent a few years ago in the middle of a Little League baseball game.

We have three children. At the time of this particular incident, our oldest son, Andrew, was eleven. We've taught our kids that sports are not just about sports. They're about looking for opportunities to connect with people who are disconnected from God. The ballpark is our mission field. But, like any parent, we love to watch our kids compete. And we love to watch them win. But we believe there is a larger context to the game.

We've taught our kids that sports are not just about sports. They're about looking for opportunities to connect with people who are disconnected from God. The ballpark is our mission field.

During this particular baseball season, Andrew wasn't getting much playing time, only a couple of innings in left or right field and then back on the bench. The coaches would promise him innings at the beginning of a game and then leave him on the bench. These particular coaches were not among my favorites. Still, Andrew handled the whole thing pretty well.

After placing first and second in a couple of tournaments, Andrew's team was guaranteed an invitation to the state tournament. So for all practical purposes, the pressure was off. We had a couple of games coming up that didn't really matter. It was during the second of those games that things came to a head.

It was the top of the sixth inning in a six-inning game. We were the home team and losing 12–3. Andrew had been on the bench the entire game. There was no way we were coming back. Again, this game didn't count. It was the type of situation where a good coach puts in the players who don't get a lot of field time. And sure enough, the head coach finally put Andrew in. He was in left field, but at least he was *on* the field. And since he was on the field, he was in the batting rotation.

After three quick outs, we were up to bat for the last time in the game. Andrew was on deck getting ready to hit when the head coach made a last-minute change, pulling Andrew out of the batting order and sending him back to the dugout. It was so ridiculous that even the coach's wife headed to the dugout to express her dismay. But I wasn't dismayed. I was angry. Real angry. As angry as I've ever been in my life. If you have kids, you know the depth of anger a father is capable of feeling when he sees his child hurt. Especially when an adult causes the hurt.

As Andrew trotted back to the dugout, I got up and left the bleachers. I walked around to the other side of the backstop beyond the bleachers of the opposing team and stood there looking into our team's dugout at the face of my very disappointed son. While clutching the chain-link fence, I started having imaginary conversations with the coach. I'll spare you the specifics. You can imagine. Don't factor in that I'm a pastor. I wasn't having a pastoral conversation. It was anything but that.

Just as it was getting juicy, I heard a voice behind me say, "Andy?"

I turned around and faced a big guy wearing a baseball cap and shorts. "Yeah," I said, not very graciously.

He introduced himself and it was obvious he wanted to talk. I wasn't interested in talking. I was in the middle of an imaginary conversation with Andrew's coach. Not only that, the game was about to end and I needed to get back to the dugout, rescue my son, and have a real conversation with his coach. But this guy went right on.

"I haven't attended church in years," he said. "My wife started going to North Point and loved it. Then she started inviting me."

I saw where he was headed. *Oh, no, you don't, God,* I groaned. *Uh-uh. I'm mad and I plan to stay that way for the next couple of hours. Nobody treats my son this way and gets*

away with it. I'm not going to let a story about somebody's
wife bringing him to church interfere with my mood.

But this guy went on and on about how he'd been to North Point Community Church and what a difference it was beginning to make. He told me about joining a small group with his wife. He was even contemplating joining a men's group on Friday mornings. It was a remarkable story. I should have been thrilled. But I was determined to stay angry. The longer he talked, however, the more difficult it was for me to stay disengaged. It was as if God in his grace was whispering, *"Andy, remember what you are out here for. It's not just about baseball."*

When the man finished, I shook his hand and thanked him for sharing his story. By that time some of my anger had dissipated. I walked back over to the dugout to discover that the team was planning to get ice cream after the game. The last thing I wanted to do was go out and act like everything was fine. I did my best to avoid eye contact with the coaches, herded my family to the car, loaded everybody up, and just sat there.

"Andrew, you don't want to get ice cream with the team, do you?" I asked.

"I guess not," he said quietly.

My second-born son, Garrett, picked up on our emotion and started railing on the coach. "I can't believe the coach didn't play Andrew. What's wrong with him? They weren't going to win that game anyway. Why couldn't he just play Andrew for once?"

Finally, in a moment of clarity, again by God's grace, I interrupted Garrett's tirade. "You know what? Didn't we decide at the beginning of the season that we're not here just

It was as if God in his grace was whispering, *"Andy, remember what you are out here for. It's not just about baseball."*

to play baseball? Haven't we prayed that God would help us connect with people who might be disconnected from him?"

Then I told them about my conversation with the stranger. As I described what happened, I was overwhelmed with the sense that none of this was coincidental. "I think something good will come from this. We can't quit because this isn't about baseball."

Everyone reluctantly agreed. So I started the car and we drove to the ice cream shop.

I can't tell you how much I did not want to get out of the car and see the coaches. But I got out. Before I reached the door, the assistant coach came over and started apologizing profusely for what had happened. He even went so far as to say that he disagreed with the head coach's decision to pull Andrew out of the lineup. That felt good. To Andrew's credit, he went right in and mingled with the guys as if nothing had happened. Still, I avoided the head coach, and I'm pretty sure he was avoiding me.

When we got in the car to leave, we prayed for the team, Andrew's coaches, and our influence as a family.

By the end of the state tournament, one of the coaches was attending North Point with his family on a regular basis. Three months later, he was baptized. As I mentioned earlier, our baptisms are often emotional. This one was absolutely overwhelming to Sandra and to me. Now Bob serves as a small group leader in our middle school division.

Over time, the head coach and I became friends. I've never had a conversation about spiritual matters with him. But the door is certainly open for that. It's only open, however, because by God's grace and a conversation with a stranger, I remembered that life is not about protecting my ego or staying within my comfort zone.

Years ago I embraced a vision that was broader than all of that. And I never want to have to look back and wonder what my life would have been like if I had allowed circumstances to disconnect me from my vision—from what

> If God has given
> you a picture of what could
> be and should be, embrace it
> fully and refuse to allow the
> busyness and urgency of
> life to distract you.

God called me to be and do. After the game that night, I almost made Andrew quit the team. That would have been a terrible mistake. It wasn't just a team we would have been abandoning. We would have abandoned something far more important.

It will always be difficult to make vision stick. After all, vision is about creating something new— something that should be, but won't be, without someone's dogged determination to see it through to the end. If God has given you a picture of what could be and should be, embrace it fully and refuse to allow the busyness and urgency of life to distract you. Whether it's a business, educational, or spiritual endeavor, do what it takes to make your vision stick.

Making your vision stick requires bold leadership. It will require you to develop a healthy intolerance for those things that have the potential to impede your progress. All the leaders I've met have mental pictures of what could and should be for their organizations, but not every leader is willing to pay the price to turn his or her ideas into reality. It takes more than imagination and passion to make what *could be* and *should be* into *what is*. Seeing a vision become a reality requires more than a single burst of energy or creativity. It requires daily attention. Daily commitment.

If you are consumed with the tension between *what is* and *what could be* . . . if you find yourself emotionally involved . . . frustrated . . . brokenhearted . . . maybe even angry about the way things are . . . if you believe that God is behind your anguish . . . then chances are you are on the brink of something divine, something too important to abandon.

Pay the price. Embrace the vision. And do whatever it takes to make your vision stick!

LEADERSHIP DEVELOPMENT MATTERS

The Leadership Summit, a two-and-a-half day event, convenes every August in the Chicago area and is satellite broadcast live to more than 130 locations across North America. Designed for leaders in any arena—ministry, business, nonprofit—its purpose is to encourage and equip Christian leaders with an injection of vision, skill development, and inspiration.

For up-to-date information about The Leadership Summit, visit www.willowcreek.com/summit

When Leadership and Discipleship Collide

Bill Hybels

What do you do when the laws of
leadership collide with the teachings
of Christ?

Modern business practice and
scholarship have honed the laws of leadership. To achieve
success, you're supposed to—among other things—leverage
your time, choose a strong team and avoid unnecessary
controversy. But what happens when the laws of leadership
and discipleship collide?

Using stories from his own life and ministry, Bill Hybels
shows how the laws of leadership sometimes crash
headlong into the demands of discipleship. And how the
decisions you make at that point could affect not only you,
but the destiny of those you lead.

Hardcover: 0-310-28306-X

Pick up a copy today at your favorite bookstore!

This resource was created to serve you and to help you build a local church that prevails. It is just one of many ministry tools that are part of the Willow Creek Resources® line, published by the Willow Creek Association together with Zondervan.

The Willow Creek Association (WCA) was created in 1992 to serve a rapidly growing number of churches from across the denominational spectrum that are committed to helping unchurched people become fully-devoted followers of Christ. Membership in the WCA now numbers over 12,000 Member Churches worldwide from more than ninety denominations.

The Willow Creek Association links like-minded Christian leaders with each other and with strategic vision, training and resources in order to help them build prevailing churches designed to reach their redemptive potential. Here are some of the ways the WCA does that.

The Leadership Summit—A once a year, two-and-a-half-day learning experience to envision and equip Christians with leadership gifts and responsibilities. Presented live on Willow's campus as well as via satellite simulcast to over 135 locations across North America—plus more than eighty international cities feature the Summit by way of videocast every Fall—this event is designed to increase the leadership effectiveness of pastors, ministry staff, volunteer church leaders and Christians in the marketplace.

Ministry-Specific Conferences—Throughout the year the WCA hosts a variety of conferences and training events—both at Willow Creek's main campus and offsite, across North America and around the world. These events are for church leaders and volunteers in areas such as group life, children's ministry, student ministry, preaching and teaching, the arts and stewardship.

Willow Creek Resources®—Provides churches with trusted and field-tested ministry resources on important topics such as leadership, volunteer ministries, spiritual formation, stewardship, evangelism, group life, children's ministry, student ministry, the arts and more.

WCA Member Benefits—Includes substantial discounts to WCA training events, a 20 percent discount on all Willow Creek Resources®, *Defining Moments* monthly audio journal for leaders, quarterly *Willow* magazine, access to a Members-Only section on WCA's web site, monthly communications and more. Member Churches also receive special discounts and premier services through the WCA's growing number of ministry partners—Select Service Providers—and save an average of $500 annually depending on the level of engagement.

For specific information about WCA conferences, resources, membership, and other ministry services, contact:

Willow Creek Association
P.O. Box 3188, Barrington, IL 60011-3188
Phone: 847-570-9812 • Fax: 847-765-5046
www.willowcreek.com

We want to hear from you.

Please send your comments about this book

to us in care of zreview@zondervan.com. Thank you.